THE COMPTROLLER'S COMPTROLLER: HOW I BECAME A COMPTROLLER'S COMPTROLLER
A TRUE STORY

by

CONNOR M. GLEIM

IN LOVING MEMORY OF
MARSHALL SCHLAHNG GEYER

We will never forget you. Nobody saw that sinkhole coming. I mean, you weren't surprised by it – you were trying to do cool skateboard tricks over the hole. We told you it was too wide for you to make it.

Anyway, we miss you.

TABLE OF CONTENTS

PROLOGUE

Comptrollering. That's what they call it. I prefer 'Fiscal Computing,' but I see why they don't use that term. The concept of computing — which is often reserved for what we perceive as "computers" — is exciting. It intrigues people. In fact, it intrigues me, too. I, Connor Gleim, am not a computer. I don't speak in ones and zeros. I am simply a Comptroller, albeit in private. When I'm out in public, I might as well be a computer — because people have no clue what I do. The truth is, I am a financial wizard, and I keep this town thriving, economically speaking. I run the most successful comptroller program in the entire nation, and somebody else gets all the credit. I don't mind. In a way, I like holding that secretive knowledge and power. I get paid large sums of money — more than most Comptrollers — to do what I love: fiscal computing. But to the general public: I'm a nobody. This is the personal story of my comptrollering career and how I became a comptroller's comptroller.

- Connor M. Gleim

CHAPTER 1
AT ALL COSTS

Flashing lights. That's all I saw as the crowd of 20,000 people grew more and more silent in anticipation, staring right back at me and the few others on the stage. They had a good reason to be hanging on every heartbeat we sounded, for this was the night. Election Night. And not just any election night – the City Comptroller Election Night. You see, in our town, City Comptroller might as well be the President of the United States of America. Every four years, this night is the most important event, and the 100% voting rate would agree. Heck, even the regular election night – which represents every single other position in the city government – doesn't have a 100% voting outcome. The position of City Comptroller is truly the only position that represents every single one of our town's residents.

That's why all eyes were on me – Connor Gleim – and my opponent Jack Lozenge. It was a neck-and-neck race, anybody's game. We were tied in the polls, we had an equal amount of scandals throughout the race, and we both had the grit it took to become a politician – more importantly, a comptroller. Oh! I almost forgot – there was actually one other person in this race. Gina Can- uh… something like Cannon? Gina Crayon? Oh, that's right – Gina Canyon. Aside from me and Jack Lozenge, Gina Canyon was also running for the coveted position of City Comptroller, with just one difference: she was the incumbent. Not that that title held a lot of weight for her – the general populace frequently forgot her name, her contributions, and the fact that she exists. In fact, I'm only 80% sure that her last name truly was Canyon and not, like, Candle or something like that. Nonetheless, Gina is actually the reason City Comptroller is such a highly sought-after and admired role.

During her 20 years in the position, she fixed the city up from financial despair to fiscal utopia. She handled the city's finances as if her life depended on it – generating enough money to provide Universal Basic Income to the city's residents, fix every issue from infrastructure to the housing crisis, and even put us on the map. Gina was so good at being City Comptroller that she essentially built the comptroller model for every city in the nation. The Federal Reserve and the U.S. Treasury even mimic the way Gina ran our town. Because of her great money management skills and ability to build a system that works for an entire nation, Gina eventually won a FUCC Award. That's right – the Federal Union of City Comptrollers honored Gina Canyon with the Mr. Moneybags Star Comptroller award in 2009, which was unsurprising to pretty much everyone in the nation.

However, Gina did not matter in the City Comptroller race against me and Jack. You see, while she was one of the most successful politicians our town and nation had ever seen, she had such an unforgettable face and a personality made from the sensation you receive when you watch paint dry or grass grow. It's not that she was unlikable, it was more so that she held the air of someone who is less than an extra in a movie – if that's even possible. She was the type of person who might pass you on a hike in the middle of the Sahara Desert, and you would have sworn you saw nobody along your path at the end of the day. If she is dead now – a possible fact of which I do not know – surely the newspaper editor would forget to print her obituary, not that it would have changed the readership count. In fact, this is probably the most that has ever been written about Gina Canvas.

After 20 years, Gina finally had an opponent in the City Comptroller race. Two, at that. And the election night came down to either me, the beloved Connor Gleim whom the city had admiration for (with much thanks to the wife), or Jack Lozenge. With as many flashing lights as there were that night, you'd think that the winner of the race was Electromagnetic Radiation. But just as we were blinded by the rays, and deafened by the silence of the crowd awaiting voting results, Kim began to speak.

"Hello everyone. As the designated elections announcer, I want to remind you all how hard we have been working that poll. You'll remember that, in an attempt to make the voting process a little more lively, we constructed flash mob events at all polling locations across the city. And boy did we dance those polls. I want to thank all of you, especially the ones who donated by tossing dollar bills at our dancers and screaming, 'Get it, shawty.' We're not entirely sure what you meant, but your contributions made this election night possible.

"And without further ado, I will open this envelope and announce the winner of our city's next Comptroller. And the winner is..."

$ $ $

bzzzz Oh, how I remember the sound of that alarm clock. The alarm clock that woke me up every day of the election cycle – a total of 90 days. And this was the first. I opened my eyes and threw the covers off of my energized and well-rested being. I was awake – alive! Time to start the race. I unplugged my phone from the charger sitting in the socket underneath my huge windows that overlooked the city. I took a deep look out, a deep breath in, and got ready to call my Campaign Intern, Bartosz Wiśniewski. "I'm coming for you, City," I mumbled to my gaze as I dialed Bartosz' number. I had to consult the piece of paper I had laying on my desk to remember his confusing phone number. *+48? He really is an exchange student, huh?* I thought to myself as I punched in the rest of the digits.

"Wit- I mean, Hello!" Bartosz stated, almost as if it was a matter of fact, after answering the phone immediately.

"Bartosz! I hope you're ready for the fun to begin. Today is the day! I know you're not from the United States, but you're in for one hell of a ride. Trust that!" I assured him in a tone that would scare him only a little. I needed someone who was buckled down for the ride, and who wouldn't ask to be removed. I didn't care that he was from somewhere in Central Europe that I forgot the name of – he was a Political Science major at one of the most prestigious universities in this nation, so he had to do.

"Mr. Gleim, I promise to do my best and provide you with the best campaign management out of every candidate!" he beamed.

"Okay, calm down. Call me Connor. And I don't need you to be the best – just don't chicken out halfway through. I need you to understand that City Comptroller is the most important position in this town, and as such the race will come down to much more than a strong campaign manager. It will come down to scandals, public relations, populace manipulation, and pure grit."

There was a significant pause before Bartosz finally asked, "… Is that our platform?"

"Wha- No! This is all off the record. Anything – and I mean *anything* – I tell you on calls is off the record. That means it should not be repeated to the other candidates, the press, or anyone. Understood?"

"Understood. What about in person?"

"What?"

"Well, you said anything said to me on phone calls is off the record... What about things you say to me in person?"

"Shut up, Bartosz. Just don't repeat anything I say unless I give you explicit permission. Got it?"

"Got it. Okay, what's the first order of business? Day one means submitting the campaign materials, right?"

"Correct. Email the materials to Kim. She's the Head Poll Worker and the Designated Elections Official. Carefully re-read the instructions I gave you and then send her an email with the Campaign Marketing Materials and the Campaign Social Media Accounts. That should be it for today. This is just the beginning, so make sure you take one of the only breaths you'll be afforded during the next three months." I was probably sounding a bit harsh and scary at this point, but I needed to be sure he was ready.

"Will do, Mr. Gle- I mean, Connor!" Bartosz announced.

We said our goodbyes and I got ready for the day before heading downstairs. Along the way I passed my daughter, Margaret's room and noticed she was just waking up. Like father, like daughter. Except she wasn't waking up to the most important day of her life! However, if there was a City Comptroller election for 4-year-olds, I'm sure she would be a shoe-in. She was the smartest and most dedicated student in her pre-school class, awarding her Ms. Congeniality at the end-of-the-year class awards and 'Most Likely To Be Kindergarten President' in the yearbook superlatives. *But there won't be a Kindergarten Award ceremony if I don't get elected City Comptroller*, I thought to myself. The City Education Department was strapped for funding and had to decide which schools deserved to stay open. Future University Kids of Kindergarten (FUKK) was at the top of the department's list for slashing funding thanks to the student suicide rate correlating to the tough curriculum and militant-style learning philosophy. But I wanted the best for my little Marge. *I must win.*

"Daddy? What are you doing standing there?" Marge asked as she pulled me out of my own head.

"Hi, honey. I was just coming by to take you down to breakfast. Are you ready for your last day of school?" I asked as I helped her gather her backpack and school items.

"I don't want school to end," she said with a sad voice and tears in her eyes. "I'm scared of going to FUKK."

"It's all right, honey. You still have the whole summer to prepare. You have those FUKK study cards I got you for your birthday, right?"

"Yes, but they're too hard. I don't even know what Cacku-calchu-catchulus is."

"It's pronounced *Calculus*, Marge, and it'll help you get university ready! After Kindergarten starts primary school. And then secondary school is right around the corner. Before you know it, you'll need to focus on your higher education, and you can't do that without attending the absolute best Kindergarten in the nation. Now brush your teeth and come downstairs – your mother made your favorite breakfast."

"Croquembouche?!" Marge screamed before sporting a smile that connected one ear to the other.

"Don't be silly! Croquembouche is not a breakfast item!" She always had a way to make me laugh.

I left my detour and finally headed to the kitchen, where Misty was expelling the most exquisite scents with each whisk and flip. That was her best feature really: she was the best cook on this side of the tracks! I just wish I had appreciated that a bit more. After I ghostwrote Nicholas Walsh's book, things started to go downhill. I mean, for me personally, things went uphill – I had just ghostwritten the most important book of the 21st century, my career soared higher than ever imagined, and the United States Government awarded me with a Purple Heart (the first instance of a civilian receiving one). Unfortunately, that meant I needed more time away from Misty and Marge, something Misty didn't take too well. I thought the six-figure income, the trips around the world, and the many extra diamond heart pendants (her favorite!) would offset the negatives effects of me being gone for up to 95% of each year. But I don't think they were enough.

I must win City Comptroller... to save my

marriage, I thought to myself before gathering up the courage to walk into the kitchen. It's not that I was nervous or afraid to be around Misty, it's just that she had a way of placing the blame on me. The blame for what, you ask. Anything! I'm the reason the dog shits on the carpet. I'm the reason the birds chirp too early in the morning. I'm the reason her grandmother died last year (okay, maybe that last one was true, but how was I supposed to know she was allergic to parsnips?).

"Hey dear! It smells de-lic-ious! I can't wait for some of your famous breakfast sausages," I beamed as I went in to give her a hug.

"Well these aren't for you, Connor. They are for Margaret. She absolutely must have the perfect last day of school. I don't want her freaking out about attending FUKK next year. I'm sorry, but you'll have to make your own breakfast," Misty shot back, expectedly.

I should've just jumped out my windows this morning – at least that would've hurt less than this attitude. "That's okay, dear. I'll just throw something together. Oh, and I just spoke with Marge. She's almost done getting ready and she's in a better mindset about her academic future than she was when she woke up," I offered, careful not give any attitude back. Lest we get into one of our common fights that ended with me sleeping at the local airport motel again. "Happy first day of campaigning, right?"

"Ugh, I was hoping you'd have come to your senses and dropped out by now. WHY must you always be busy? I thought you promised me you would make yourself more available to me and Margaret?"

"No, I promised you that I would give up Ghostwriting in order to stay put. But what do you expect me to do with that – stay home 24/7 and never have a life again? The campaign is only three months long, and it's much harder and more time-consuming than the position of City Comptroller itself. After I win, I'm all yours. And remember: I'm doing this partially for you. You *know* your favorite brunch place – Food UnCorked! – is at risk of going out of business if they don't receive that government loan, which will be decided by the next City Comptroller," I pleaded.

"You know I don't like giving you credit, but I do want to save FUC from going under.

Fine. Have a great first day of campaigning, but don't expect my support. I'll be spending the whole summer helping Margaret practice her FUKK study cards anyway."

Suddenly the sound of feet flying across the house filled our ears. "I heard my name!!!!" Marge exclaimed as she jumped into her seat at the breakfast table. "What were you guys talking about??"

"Oh nothing, honey. I was just getting ready to go down to the campaign office and telling your mother goodbye," I explained, happy to have a reason to leave. I hated fighting with Misty in front of our daughter – nothing good could come of that.

"Bye-bye, daddy. I'll eat a sausage for you!" Marge stated innocently.

"Thank you, honey! Make sure you check it for any parsnips – you don't want to end up like your great-grandmother!" I said as I shot darts at Misty with my eyes. I shut the door as fast as I could and rushed to my car before any trouble ensued.

Just as I opened the car door, I received a call from a number that could only be Bartosz'. *Why is he calling me? Shouldn't he be knee-deep in sending an email to Kim?* "Hello?" I answered.

"C-Connor. There's… there's something wrong with our campaign social media accounts," Bartosz said in a scared tone.

"What do you mean something wrong?"

"Well, I went to log into the campaign Twitter account to prepare it for Kim, and there was a private message waiting for us in the inbox," he continued as if waiting long enough would soften the blow he was expecting.

"And? What did it say?"

"You'll have to see this for yourself, Connor. I'm not sure how to convey it with my limited English."

"Bartosz, you're awfully suspenseful, you know that? Just tell me: does Kim have our campaign materials or not?"

"No, that's the thing, Connor – I can't possibly send over the materials without figuring out this message first. Kim will know something's up, and I don't want to be the cause of your first scandal of the election season. I think it's best if you come over and advise me of the situation," Bartosz said in a tone that bordered on confusion and dread.

"Fine, I'll be right there."

CHAPTER 2
HACKS ON HACKS

"Okay explain to me what's going on," I started as I walked into Bartosz' 150x150 square foot studio apartment.

"Connor- You didn't even knock. What if I would have been eating my Pierogi and watching the newest episode of 'ŚLEPNĄC OD ŚWIATEŁ'?" Bartosz said in a confused state.

"I have no idea what you're talking about, per usual. Anyway, hurry up – explain to me what this campaign social media account situation is, and why you can't send the accounts over to Kim yet. I have a game of golf I need to prepare for at 4 PM," I said in a rushed manner.

"Well, Connor... It seems we have a hacker."

"What does that even mean?"

"A hacker is someo-"

"No, Bartosz, I KNOW what a hacker is. What did they hack? What are they asking for? What do they have ahold of? What are the details?" I was getting real tired of my valuable golf time being taken up.

Bartosz looked scared. I decided to let up the attitude a little bit. "Okay, just tell me what we need to do. We'll make it a quick fix and then we can both go on with our days. The first day is supposed to be the easiest."

"The hacker has hold of all of our social media accounts, but they're only reaching out via Twitter direct message. I think you better just read the message for yourself – it's quite long and says things that I don't fully understand," Bartosz explained.

"Okay, pull it up. I don't have experience with Twitter, so you'll have to show me the message."

Bartosz pulled up the direct message, enlarged it, then turned the computer screen toward me.

To the Campaign Officials of
Connor M. Gleim,
City Comptroller Candidate:

Connor, I know what you did last summer. You think you're so sly, don't you? Big ghostwriting figurehead, multi-millionaire traveler, City Comptroller hopeful. You think you have it all figured out — that you have it all. You're invincible and nothing can touch you, huh? Well I'm here to change all of that. You're probably wondering who I am. I won't dwell on any details that don't pertain to what I'm here to do. We'll have to discuss my identity another day. And trust me, there will be other days. You won't get rid of me easily.

"You were a ghostwriter?" Bartosz interrupted.

"Bartosz, shut up — I'm trying to read. And yes, I was the most famous Ghostwriter in the nation, and I traveled the world teaching ghostwriting seminars."

"Why didn't you ever come to Poland?"

"I don't even know where that is," I said

before I continued to read.

I have hacked all of your campaign social media accounts. I have access to your email address, your phone records, and your web search history. I have everything. Don't try to delete it — I made a copy, and a copy of that copy. Or I guess do delete it if you want — it just won't matter to me. I have it all. Don't worry though, I won't leak anything if you comply with my demands:

1. *Don't say anything about this message or the fact that you were hacked. You're going to send your campaign social media accounts and marketing materials to Kim, no questions asked. She won't know they've been hacked unless you say otherwise.*

2. *You're going to do what I say, when I say it. Don't worry — I won't make you do anything obscene or dangerous. I'm not here to ruin your life or make a mockery of ethical hacking. The only way your life will be ruined is if you decide to tell anyone about this little message. What I will ask of you will be strictly related to the*

election. Don't try any funny business. You better conduct this campaign along election guidelines and in a fair manner.

3. Don't accuse another candidate of hiring me. I have hacked every single candidate, and have more than ample information that would lead to each of your disqualification. Don't believe me? You'll soon find out just how serious I am.

Good luck, Connor. I sincerely hope this election turns out how you might want. However, I have a feeling that is highly unlikely. For all of you.

- ☺ Anonymous ☺

"Connor... what's the dirt he has on you?" Bartosz asked with a tone that suggested he might be too nervous to continue working on the campaign.

As I was coming out of my shocked state, I barely caught Bartosz' question. "Oh, nothing important. You know, as a ghostwriter, I have a lot of confidential clients who may not want the general public knowing that they hired someone to write their book for them," I said as quickly as I had thought of it.

"But... why would that be grounds for disqualification? You said everyone knows you as a famous ghostwriter – so doesn't Kim already know all of that?" Bartosz annoyingly questioned.

"Sure, I guess. I don't know, Bartosz. Maybe the hacker doesn't know that? I'm not worried about it – just get the accounts over to Kim and let's move on with the campaign. You have nothing to worry about," I retorted in an attempt to persuade him to stay on board with the campaign. But I had something to worry about. I knew exactly what dirt the hacker had on me. And it would definitely put a dent in my life as I knew it.

"Connor, it's 3:52 PM..." Bartosz mumbled as I was thinking to myself.

I looked down at my watch. "SHIT! Okay, hold off on sending the accounts. We have until Midnight anyway. Let's go!"

"Wait, when was I suddenly invited? I have a Public Health class to study for. The exam is tomorr-" Bartosz attempted to say.

"I need a ball retriever and I don't have time to check one out at the country club now that you've made me late. You'll have to do it. Bring your notes and study them on the course."

"Connor, do you really think now is the best time to be golfing?"

"All of my funders and supporters will be there. I know it may seem silly to someone from another country, but in the United States of America, we don't back down from a game of golf. That's a surefire way of depleting your funding sources and losing your supporters. Now grab my golf bag that I brought in here for some reason. We only have five minutes to rush over!"

$ $ $

"Well if it isn't Connor Gleim being fashionably late, per usual. What, the campaign got you tied up already? I thought the first day was supposed to be the easiest!" said a familiar voice as Connor and Bartosz walked inside the Frank Ufford Country Club.

Great. If it isn't Chalmers Topaz, the richest man in town. And he hasn't declared his allegiance to my campaign yet. I knew it was a long shot, but what gives with this guy? Why show up to my benefit game of golf without explicit support? I thought to myself before giving him a hearty handshake.

"I'm just messing with you, chap. I didn't get to where I am today by making it on time to golf games at FUCC. You gotta show them who they're waiting for!" Chalmers said through a smile on his face. "And who is this young lad?"

"Oh, this is Bartosz. He's my campaign manager, but he's actually just here as my golf retrieval boy. I imagine the club's boys are all checked out by now. Either way, it'll be good for him to get a sense of what a benefit game is like. He's new to the states and doesn't know much about U.S. politics. Isn't that right, Bartosz?" I said with a nudge.

"Hi. I'm Bartosz. I'm very grateful for the opportunity to work with Connor on his race to become the next City Comptroller, and for my first time being here at FUCC. Not to be rude, but are you one of the supporters? I don't recognize you from the database."

"Ha ha, no, son. Not yet, at least. I'm keeping my options open. My name is Chalmers Topaz and I carry a huge weight in the way this town votes. Money talks, after all," Chalmers retorted with his smile turning into a grin. "Let's see if Connor can beat me in a game of golf – then you'll know if I'm a supporter or not!" Chalmers turned his gaze to me, once again. "Say, Connor, where'd you get this boy anyway? He looks to be about 17 years old – shouldn't he be doing chores at home or something?"

"He's 21, and he's a Political Science major at the top of his class at Politics & Humanities Undergraduate College. He helped me at the local Walmart and we got to talking about his aspirations. I felt he would be the best candidate for the job given his youthful motivation and desire for a summer internship," I explained.

Chalmers turned back to Bartosz. "Oh PHUC! I graduated from there! Class of '89, to be exact. Well, I will say, they have the most extensive Political Science program. With that, coupled with this internship, I'd say you're on track to become City Comptroller yourself one day, young lad," Chalmers said with a chuckle. "Anyway, I'll let you two be. I gotta go warm up my back-swing!"

Bartosz turned to me and asked, "Who was that?"

"Chalmers… were you not listening, Bartosz?"

"No, I know his name. But there was a strange aura about him. I couldn't tell if you guys liked each other or not," Bartosz admitted.

"Well, all I can say is that I'll have an answer for you on that by the end of the night," I said as I kept a watchful eye on Chalmers. "We'll see."

"I don't get it. Why is he at our benefit game if he's not yet a supporter? I thought they were only letting funders and supporters in tonight," Bartosz pondered.

"When you're the richest guy in town, you can get in anywhere, Bartosz. Also, he's the Godfather of the LaQuinta Airport Motel heiress, Barcelona LaQuinta. And the Airport Motel arm of LaQuinta just happens to be catering this event tonight. Otherwise, he wouldn't have even known about it. I'll let you in on a secret: he has no intention of backing my campaign. He's been buddy-buddy with my running mate, Jack Lozenge, for years. In fact, I'm pretty sure Chalmers is the reason Jack is running. I'm not sure of the connection yet, but I just know some colluding is going on. I'm not comfortable with him being here, but I do know how faithful he is to a game of golf. If I beat him, he will 100% back my campaign. But that's next to impossible," I explained to Bartosz.

"That all sounds rather confusing. I hope it all connects by the end of this boo- I mean, election cycle," Bartosz responded.

"What?"

"What?"

"Oh, dang it – Kim is calling me. Did you send her the campaign materials yet?"

"No, you told me to do it later because we had to hurry here," Bartosz explained.

"Okay, I'll just let her know we're preparing them now. Go to the FUCC Business Center and log into the accounts. I'll let you know when to send them over. We still have a bit of time before the golf game begins," I said to

Bartosz before answering Kim's call.

"Kim! Heyyyy, how are you?" I asked nervously.

"I'm okay, Connor. Look, I know you're busy with your campaign benefit kickoff night, but the election committee really needs your campaign social media accounts and marketing materials before midnight. I'm only letting you know this early because we've already received the campaign materials from Jack Lozenge, Montgomery O'Donnell, and uh… the other one."

"Gina?"

"Oh, yes. Gina Cannabis. Anyway, just get your materials in as soon as you can. I don't want to have to disqualify you for something as silly as neglecting an email on the first day of the race," Kim stated in a stern tone.

"Will do, Kim. I'm sending Bartosz off to do it now. You'll get those materials before I can finish saying 'Connor Gleim Is The Next City Comptroller!'," I joked as I motioned to Bartosz to send the email.

"You better say it slower then. Have a great night," Kim said before hanging up.

I walked over to the business center and

found Bartosz clicking send on the campaign materials.

"All done, Connor! Kim has the accounts and materials, and now we can focus on having a relaxing benefit dinner," Bartosz said happily.

"Let's hope."

We walked outside to a crowd of people watching as Chalmers got ready for the big game. Everyone cheered as I entered the golf course and shook his hand. They were there to see me, after all.

"Good luck, son," Chalmers said in an almost-threatening tone. He then handed me a golf club out of the LaQuinta sponsored Sunday bag.

I motioned to him that I had my own bag and then took out my lucky golf club. It was a gift from the Dalai Lama after I ghostwrote his book The Art of Happiness. I took a deep breath, prayed into the golf club, and then stepped up to the golf ball.

As I began to swing, an emergency alert tone blasted through the course. Everyone's phones were going off with the same ear-shattering tone. We all knew this could mean only one thing: mandatory town meeting.

"Better luck next time," Chalmers said to me as we rushed to get off the course and over to the Town Rhombus, where all town meetings, election debates, and festivities commenced.

As I rushed out of the building, I noticed Bartosz still in the business center playing on the computer. "Come on, Bartosz! We gotta go. Stop playing computer games. Didn't you hear the cacophony of emergency noises?" I yelled over to him.

"Sorry, Connor. I was busy studying for my exam tomorrow – I guess I was in a state of flow. Is everything okay?"

"No, Bartosz. Everyone in the town just received an emergency text that stated we need to head to the Town Rhombus immediately."

"Oh, I guess my komórka didn't receive the message because it's from Poland."

"Just get in my car and let's go," I said while rushing him outside of the building.

We jumped inside my car and sped toward the center of the city. *This better not be connected to that hacker*, I thought to myself, being careful not to say anything out loud, lest Bartosz finds out I actually do have a secret the hacker could use against me.

$$\$ \ \$ \ \$$

"Welcome everyone. I'm glad to see all 20,000 of you could make it," Kim said into a microphone on a podium set up in the upper right corner of the Town Rhombus.

"What's going on?? Tell us what's happening! Is there a natural disaster? Another pandemic scare?" people began asking left and right. Everyone was standing uneasy, bracing for what they believed would be the worst news. All ears were on Kim.

Kim quickly hushed the crowd with two claps of her hands. The crowd clapped back. Kim moved the microphone closer to her face and said, "If I can have everyone's attention. Please listen closely. I'm afraid this emergency is much worse than what you're suspecting."

People broke their silence to gasp and murmur to the person next to them. All sorts of theories were being thrown about – Aliens, President Assassination, Secret Tunnels, etc. The noise level rose with fear – and a little bit of excitement, to be honest – but Kim reeled everyone back in.

"It appears one of our City Comptroller candidates is in hot water. I apologize, but there may have to be a disqualification tonight."

Screams shattered eardrums across the town. The tears of our residents dripped from their faces, creating a pool of sorrow and disappointment below them. One person even slipped and had to be taken to the emergency room. People began consoling each other, questioning authority, rioting, and gathering their own composure. It was almost as if the whole town was going through the steps of grief at the same time. It got to the point where the only way to get everyone's attention was to sound the emergency alarm again.

"I know this comes as a disgusting, heart-wrenching shock to all of us. We all believe in the position of City Comptroller and would defend it with our own life. I feel the same way. I am just as torn apart and angered as you are. Trust me, being alone with the news for the past hour did not do well for my mental health. I'm sure you're all wondering which candidate is potentially being disqualified and what they did to deserve it. If I can have all four candidates come up to the stage and stand behind me," Kim said with tears and madness in her eyes. "Montgomery O'Donnell, Jack Lozenge, Connor Gleim, and Gina Carpenter."

The town watched as each of us headed to the stage slowly, as if believing that taking caution in our steps would ensure we weren't the one being disqualified. I was the last to make it up those steps to the stage. I could feel all eyes on us, like darts getting ready to head for whoever caused this whole mess. I took my place at the left-most part of the group. We stood in a straight, horizontal line, as if we were school children awaiting our punishment from the teacher. Even though we had just arrived on stage, it felt like centuries since we had been up there. Each millisecond Kim waited to announce the culprit felt like complete agony. But I couldn't show the crowd I was on the verge of sweating – I knew the hacker had something on me that might cause disqualification, but the crowd and Kim didn't know about the hacker. And Bartosz thought I was innocent – I couldn't let him down. At least I took solace in knowing that the three people standing next to me were all feeling the same way, as they received the same message from the hacker.

"Let's start with announcing who this meeting is for, shall we?" Kim said in a sadistic tone, as if she was actually enjoying this form of public humiliation.

I squeezed my eyes real tight, grasped my hands together, and softly whispered inside my own head, *Please don't be me, please don't be me, please don't be me.*

"Montgomery O'Donnell," Kim finally announced.

Oh thank you, THANK YOU, I screamed inside of my own head as I opened up my eyes again and turned them to my opponent who was just put up for possible disqualification.

Montgomery looked terrified. Tears were

streaming down his face, but they looked like they had been coming for much longer than the announcement, as if he knew this is what the town was meeting about.

"Montgomery, would you like to tell the town what you did, or should I?" Kim asked while holding a piece of paper with the leaked information undoubtedly on it.

"I will," he said as he composed himself and walked up to the announcer podium. He replaced Kim at the microphone and tried to speak before the crowd threw a ton of 'BOO's and 'YOU SUCK's at him.

Kim stepped back up to the microphone to warn the crowd that their rowdiness would not be tolerated, and to save it for after Montgomery's announcement. Then they would be able to say what they'd like, and vocally vote on his disqualification.

"Th-thank you, Kim," Montgomery said as he stepped back up to the microphone. Kim ignored him and walked back to the other candidates. Montgomery began his announcement:

"Hi everyone. I know I'm public enemy

number one now, but please hear me out. As you may know, tonight my autobiography launched at my campaign benefit kickoff. It's only $21.99 and you can get a copy at Three Rivers Bookstore right up the street. If you buy one, make sure to take a picture of you holding it up, tweet it, and caption it '#MontgomeryForCityComptroller'.

"Anyway, I received an anonymous email earlier from someone who hacked all of my campaign accounts. The hacker admitted they knew a secret only I, and one other, knew about my book. And tonight, the rest of you will know, too. It's no secret I coordinated the release of my autobiography with the start of the City Comptroller election – I knew it would create buzz around my campaign and earn me more votes. It has been a pleasure being this town's premiere Consultant at O'Donnell's Consulting Firm, and I have had the immense pleasure helping all of you with your consulting needs. I made <u>Up Until Now: The Unbelievably True Life Story of Montgomery O'Donnell</u> to showcase the gratitude I have for this town welcoming my consulting passion into its arms.

"However, I can't say I *wrote* the book. That is why we are all here. I hired a ghostwriter to write my *auto*biography and lied about writing it myself again and again. To each and every one of you. I know lying in relation to the position of City Comptroller is the worst act one can commit in this town. And all I can say is I'm sorry."

The town collectively gasped louder than the screeches they emitted earlier. This came as a complete shock, especially because almost all 20,000 of them had bought Montgomery's book. Most of them were clutching onto their copy as he was admitting his sin. In fact, his supporters' disappointment was the loudest. They began screaming and throwing his book at him while he was still on stage. It didn't help that he was considered the front-runner and clear choice to replace Gina Candy as City Comptroller.

Thousands of book went flying towards the stage, each page dancing as they aimed for Montgomery's skin. He let out screams of pain and agony as he ran off the stage and away from the Town Rhombus. It was clear that the town agreed he should be disqualified – there was no question about it.

Me and the, now, two other candidates rushed off stage to avoid the paper bullets and inevitable paper cuts. As we gathered behind the stage, I grabbed Jack Lozenge with a vendetta in my eyes.

"I know it was you," I said in an accusatory tone.

"Why, Connor, I don't know what you mean," Jack said with a chuckle in his mouth, waiting to come up like a cat with a hairball.

"Don't play dumb with me, Jack. We all know getting Montgomery out of the race not only eliminates the clear frontrunner, but also paves the way for your 3-ring binder company – Paper Hardware and Utilities Complete – to increase the sales it's been lacking for years. You know damn well that Montgomery's consulting firm advised Gina CannedYams and her City Comptrollering office to move from physical paperwork to digital paperwork. That must have taken a huge toll on PHUC, huh? Don't pretend I don't know that if you win, you'll require that all of the financial documents in the city be reverted back to hard copies. It's just a money game to you, isn't it?"

"Fine, you caught me, Connor. But don't pretend that the hacker doesn't have something on you. If I were you, I'd be careful telling anyone of my motivations. You wouldn't want to be disqualified next, would you?" Jack said with a laugh.

"I knew it – you definitely have something to do with the hacking! Did you hire a hacker on the dark web? You won't get away with this, Jack Lozenge!" I said as quietly, but as threateningly, as I could.

"Good luck proving that. I will neither confirm nor deny," Jack said with as much confidence as he could muster up. It was clear he was attempting to a be a man of few words.

"Why do you even need your 3-ring binder company anyway? Your grandfather – Elias Loejzunjn – is the creator of the modern medical miracle, the Throat Lozenge. You know he would make you President and CEO of the company, and then you wouldn't have to worry about PHUC."

"Don't be silly, Connor. Throat Lozenges

are my grandfather's passion. 3-ring binders are my passion. I'm done talking now. Good luck figuring everything out. In the meantime, make sure your secret doesn't get leaked. Three remain," Jack said mysteriously before he walked into the dark of the night.

CHAPTER 3
EMBEZZLING EMOTIONS

After that hellish town meeting, I decided to grab Bartosz and head to the local diner. He was sitting by some steps going over flashcards for his exam tomorrow, completely oblivious to what had just happened on the stage. We walked over to Patty's Home Plate in silence – him still studying, and me trying to process all of the new election information that went down in the past 12 hours. First, my campaign accounts got hacked. Second, Chalmers showed up to my campaign benefit kickoff to offer his support in a game we ended up canceling. Third, a candidate was disqualified from the race. And then, another candidate implied he might be behind the hacking and the disqualification. It was all too much to take it.

"So much for the first day of the campaign being the easiest," I thought to myself.

"What?" Bartosz responded.

Shit, I must have said that out loud, I actually thought to myself. "Nothing, Bartosz. I hope you're getting enough studying done. This day needs to turn out productive for at least one of us."

"Actually, studying inside an environment of chaos helps me focus more, so this is better than if I were to have stayed home. Thanks for inviting me, Connor! I'm not entirely sure what's been going on all day, but it sounds bad. Where are we headed to anyway?" he asked.

"We're going to best late night diner in town: Patty's Home Plate. You'll love it there. I'm pretty sure they have pierogi. That's the ONE thing I know about your country," I responded.

"OH, that'll make me feel right at home back in Poland. Studying and pierogi – my favorite! Is there a reason we're going out to eat after all that has happened, instead of just going home and preparing the campaign for the next three months?"

"I have a feeling we'll meet someone we need to talk to there. You're about to learn a lot more information on American politics tonight, Bartosz. This is a crash course in how we do things in the United States – something to supplement your degree," I explained as I prayed for things to work out tonight and for the rest of the election cycle.

We arrived at the diner and I saw exactly who I was looking for – as expected. Bartosz and I walked up to a booth and sat down, right across from none other than…

"Montgomery! How's it going?" I asked, startling him.

"Connor, Bartosz… What are y'all doing here? Did you not witness what happened just 30 minutes ago? You better not be caught with me or people are going to talk," Montgomery said in a melancholy tone, taking time away from applying bandages to his plethora of papercuts to greet us.

"Montgomery, I know you were threatened by a hacker and that they ultimately leaked the secret about you hiring a ghostwriter. I just wanted to come by to offer my emotional support and let you know that you don't have to feel bad about what you did," I said as I saw Bartosz open up his study notes out of the corner of my eye. *Oh good, I can probably be honest with Montgomery now — there's no chance of Bartosz hearing me while he's studying.* "Hey, Montgomery?"

He looked up from applying his bandages and somberly responded, "Yes?"

"How exactly did the hacker find out your secret? I assume I got the same message you did, and I was instructed that my secret would only be leaked if I were to tell someone about the message. Did you tell someone?" I asked earnestly.

"No, that's the thing, Connor. I didn't tell a soul. I didn't even have time to tell anyone because I received the message right before my campaign benefit kickoff. And to be honesty, I forgot about it by the time the festivities commenced. It wasn't until Kim said someone might be disqualified at the town meeting that I remembered the message. I truly told no one," Montgomery admitted.

"Hmm, that's weird. The hacker even went

on a rant about 'ethical hacking' – I assumed that meant they would actually play by the rules. Wait... rules! Montgomery, the hacker gave us a list of conditions to abide by; not telling anyone about the message was just *one* of the conditions. What were the others-" I attempted to ask.

"Do what the hacker wants, when they want," a familiar voice interrupted. Montgomery and I looked up for our eyes to discover none other than Gina... whatever her last name is. She must have seen the shock on our faces as we realized we were blabbering about confidential information in a public setting. "Don't worry, I got the same message and I'm not in the business of trying to lose my job of 20 years. But keep it down, won't ya?"

"Gina, what are you doing here?" Montgomery and I said at the same time.

"Montgomery was disqualified 30 minutes ago, and he was the clear frontrunner. Shouldn't you be home celebrating?" I asked.

"Well, to go back to your pondering on how Montgomery's secret might have leaked, I fear whoever's behind the hacking – or more likely whoever hired the hacker — is not interested in playing by the rules they set forth to us. That's why I came here: I wanted to consult with the only other people I can relate to about this message. We have to figure out why Montgomery's secret was leaked despite following all the rules. Now, Montgomery, did the hacker ask you to do anything that you might have accidentally ignored?" Gina asked.

"N- no. I promise. You can look at my campaign account messages, if you want. I didn't tell anyone about the message from the hacker and I didn't fail to do anything they requested — again, I didn't even have enough time to get a request from them!" he explained.

"Wait... wasn't there a third condition?" I asked, kicking myself for not memorizing these earlier.

Gina scoffed. "Well, unlike you two, I actually remember the whole message. There was one last rule: Don't accuse another candidate of hiring the hacker. You didn't do that, right Montgomery?" she asked.

My eyes got real wide and everyone's focus at the table shifted to me. "No... but I did," I admitted. My mind began racing. *Shit, I JUST accused Jack Lozenge of hiring the hacker before coming here. If he truly did hire the hacker, he could easily have me disqualified after revealing my secret-*

Before I could finish my thought, my secret walked in through the door of the diner, almost serendipitously. Or... whatever the opposite of that word is.

She began walking toward our booth. I stressed a hush over the table and pointed my head toward the long, slender body walking our way. Bartosz must have sensed the grave feeling because he looked up from his notes and said, "Who is that" loud enough for the woman to hear from a couple yards away.

As she walked up, she answered him, "Barcelona LaQuinta. The one and only. Heiress to the Airport Motel arm of the LaQuinta company. Sure to leave you having a LaQuinta Day!" she announced with a giggle, a slight hop, and a tad lick of her red-stained lips.

Bartosz scratched his head out of confusion. "Just the Airport Motel portion of LaQuinta? Why wouldn't you be the heiress to the entire thing? Also, your name sounds like a branding decision. You Americans confuse me so much," he said before going back to studying.

"What is that little boy saying? Who is he??" Barcelona asked.

Montgomery and Gina chimed in, "Yeah, we assumed he was your son, Connor. Then we remembered you have a daughter and she's four-years-old..."

"That's my campaign manager – don't pay attention to him. I found him at a Walmart and that's all you need to know," I responded. "Barcelona, what are you doing here? Your Godfather was at my campaign golf tournament earlier stirring up trouble. Is this your doing?"

"Connor, you are always so paranoid," she said while giving me a nudge and a wink. "Actually, no – during the election cycle, I am not speaking with Chalmers. I have a feeling he's in cahoots with Jack Lozenge and will end up funding his campaign. You all know my rocky past with Jack. I am staying far, far away from that campaign."

"Oh, that's right – he's your ex-husband!" exclaimed Montgomery, as if a spark of realization went off in his head.

"Not ex yet," she began to explain. "We're separated, which means he's still technically the heir to the Airport Motel arm of LaQuinta. He has ample reason to want me out of the inheritance, and I'm afraid Chalmers might have those same reasons."

"But wait, why would your Godfather want to push you out of your own family business? This isn't the plot line to Inception! Wait… is it?" Montgomery asked.

"I don't know, Montgomery. Why don't you try killing yourself to see if you wake up," I retorted in an annoyed tone. I shifted my focus to Barcelona. "I'm so sorry, Barcelona — that's absolutely terrible," I said with a twinkle in my eye. "What are those reasons?"

"I don't know. I'm still piecing the puzzle together. But what I tell all of you doesn't leave this booth. It's my hope that we can all work together to get Jack disqualified next," Barcelona said before switching her gaze to me, "And then you win City Comptroller, Connor."

"*Ahem* I'm still in the race!" Gina exclaimed.

"Yeah, okay, Gina," Barcelona responded. "Anyway, I don't have much more information to share, but I'll make sure to update each of you as the race continues. We really have to take down Jack Lozenge. Oh, and Jack promised Chalmers a lifetime supply of LaQuinta branded 3-ring binders at all Airport Motel locations across the globe."

"Well, that's an important piece of information, Barcelona!" we all said in shocked unison.

"Oh yeah, I guess so!" Barcelona chirped. "Do you think that's why all this sketchy stuff is going on?"

"Yes, Barcelona, yes. We do think that," I answered for everyone at the booth, including Bartosz who had no clue what was going on from the comfort of his textbook. "That 3-ring binder supply is in the millions of dollars. Their deal is considered collusion and contribution fraud. With that kind of promise on the line, I wouldn't be surprised if Jack or Chalmers was willing to kill for the win..."

"Well, that sounds scary," Barcelona said while picking at her newly-done nails. "Anyway, me and Gina have a meeting to attend now. I might fund her campaign!" she giggled nonchalantly.

"Hon- I mean, Barcelona, *why* are you funding Gina Campervan's campaign? You *literally just* said that I was the clear winner if Jack were to get disqualified. Why would you help the clear loser out – wouldn't that just convolute the voting pool?" I questioned incredulously.

"First of all, *ouch*," Gina exclaimed. "Second of all, my last name is Canyon. C-A-N-Y-O-N. None of you people in this town ever get it correct. And I'm the one who put this town on the map with my skills in City Comptrollering!"

We all groaned in boredom. Her explanation felt like a death sentence – as if it were longer than this election cycle. Each word she uttered begged time to slow down, just like the first day of the campaign taking up the first three chapters of this book.

"Third of all, me and Barcelona agreed that the only way to beat Jack is to take all of our eggs out of one basket. Connor, what if you're the next candidate to be disqualified? What then? If you're harboring all of the non-Jack resources and then suddenly aren't in the race anymore, then he'll become the winner. We're trying to prevent that from happe-"

I interrupted Gina before she continued to talk our heads off for the rest of the election cycle. "Barcelona, can I talk with you by the salad bar real fast?"

Barcelona and I scurried over to the salad bar, which was across the room from the booth the others were sitting in.

"Connor, what are you doing? We're in public!"

"No, I don't want *that*. I need to tell you something. But you have to promise you'll keep it a secret," I told her quietly.

"Connnnorrrrr, *another* secret? I can barely keep our first one," she said while playfully poking me in the chest.

"I'm being serious, Barcelona. It actually relates to our first secret. But it's about the election... Someone's hacked all of the candidates' campaign accounts – emails, social media platforms, everything – and is threatening to disqualify us if we don't play by their rules. I don't know how to tell you this, but I think Jack and Chalmers might have something to do with it," I admitted as I realized just how messed up this entire situation was. I hadn't had time to really process it, but as I was explaining it to someone else, I started to sweat.

"Is that how Montgomery's secret got out?" she asked, picking olives out of the salad bar to snack on.

"Yes. Except, we're not sure why his secret was leaked to Kim. The hacker presented a list of conditions for us to follow in order to keep our secrets safe, and Montgomery didn't violate any of those conditions. I'm afraid whoever's behind the hacking – or whoever's hired the hacker – is not playing by the rules. There's a possibility any of the remaining candidates are next to be disqualified," I explained in a hushed hurry.

"So?"

"What do you mean *so*? Were you not just at the booth with the rest of us? Jack Lozenge will win this campaign unless we take this seriously. As I said, I really think he's behind all of this!" My voice was raising, but I kept my composure and ensured no one in the general vicinity could hear me.

"C'mon, Connor. You know we've been keeping this secret for about a year now," she said as she began to run her fingers up my arm. "You are part of the reason I separated from Jack Lozenge, after all. Now, I know he isn't aware of our little fling, but wouldn't it be fun to take *us* public?" She giggled in a way that always made me melt.

I began to pull my head closer to hers, as if my center of gravity was the entity known as Barcelona LaQuinta, until I stopped myself. "No! We can't. Especially not during the election cycle, Barce..." I found my fingers intertwined with hers as she dropped the olive she was holding. It hit the ground just as I came to my senses. "Besides, I'm still married to Misty. And we have a daughter – Marge. And a house, and a past, and a life! Everything!"

"Oh, you know she hasn't made you happy in years, Connor. Where is she now? Is she even helping you with your campaign?" She waited for me to answer. "That's what I thought. You need a real woman in your life, Connor. One who satisfies you, one who pleases you..." She leaned her mouth in to touch my right ear before seductively whispering, "One who makes you have a LaQuinta Day."

I was just about to give in to her advances before I realized we were in a public setting and not far out of sight from the booth. "Fine, if I promise you we can make our relationship public once the election is over, will you let it be for now," I begged her.

"It sounds like that's not up to me from what you're saying. Let's just hope the hacker doesn't get to you before the election ends," she said while winking. "Besides, I can wait. It's kind of fun having a dirty little secret."

"-lona! Barcel-" we heard Gina repeatedly chiming as she walked around the establishment darting her eyes in every direction.

"Oh! There you are, Barcelona! Come on – we have to discuss the details of the funding so we can update Kim on contributions before the end of the night," Gina said as she took Barcelona by the arm and led her out the door.

"Bye," I whispered as I watched the love of my life walk away. *I really hope no one saw any of that*, I thought to myself before heading back to the booth where Montgomery and Bartosz still resided. Apparently Montgomery was telling Bartosz horror stories about the ins-and-outs of American politics.

"Well good thing my exam tomorrow is over Public Health and not politics," Bartosz said as he held a look on his face that suggested he was actively changing his future inside of his head.

"Don't give my campaign manager any ideas, Montgomery. I can't have him quitting in the middle of the election cycle. We already have too many other things to deal with," I said as I rubbed my thumbs against my temples in a circular motion. "I just spoke with Barcelona and told her about the hacker."

"Connor… First you accuse Jack of being behind the hacking, and now you've told an outside party about the hacking? Are you trying to get disqualified?" Montgomery accused in disbelief.

"Wait, when did you accuse Jack of the hacking?" Bartosz asked.

"Just go back to studying for your exam

tomorrow, Bartosz."

Bartosz shrugged and dug his head back in his textbook.

"Montgomery, I'm not trying to get disqualified. I'm trying to play my cards right. If what you're saying about your disqualification is true, then the hacker is going to get me disqualified whether or not I play by the rules. And I'd rather go down having created a whole lot of havoc," I said with a grin on my face.

"Well then why *did* you tell her?" Montgomery asked.

"It's complicated. But I believe she's the one piece of this puzzle that connects everything. Without her, none of us are safe. Well, I guess you're not part of the puzzle anymore, but you get what I mean. We need to work with her – use her to our advantage," I explained carefully.

Montgomery nodded his head in agreement. "Makes sense. Man, I really wish I were still in the race so I could experience all of this excitement. Why did I have to be the first one disqualified? And now all I have are all these papercuts from my own damn book!

I guess I should get home and apply ointment to them. It's getting late anyway."

Before he could leave the table, I grabbed his arm and looked into his eyes. "Montgomery… if I win, I want you to know it'll be for you."

CHAPTER 4
MINT CONDITIONS

I stirred awake from a bad dream about my campaign and the election. I dreamt that I was the next candidate to get disqualified, but then there was a twist – Jack Lozenge got disqualified shortly after, absolving him of any guilt of hiring the hacker. I couldn't believe that my first night of the campaign ended in a dream in which I'm disqualified. It really was getting to me.

I got ready and looked at the clock. *11:48 AM already? What time did I get home? I didn't think we were at the diner THAT late*, I thought to myself.

"3AM," I heard a voice say from the other side of the room. "You got home last night –

or this morning, I should say — at 3AM!" Misty. She was furious.

"Oh, I'm sorry dear... Between all of the things that happened yesterday and hosting a campaign meeting at Patty's Home Plate afterwards, I lost track of time. But there were several others there! I promise I wasn't trying to create mischief or stay away from home. I would never intentionally miss Marge's first day of FUKK Summer Camp," I tried to explain.

"Don't bother. It started at 9:30AM — I already took her after she woke me up because *somebody* was dead asleep," she said as she rolled her eyes. "Anyway, I have to go pick her up for lunch time in a couple minutes, so just have fun with your campaign. And whatever you were up to last night... I will find out about it," she threatened.

"Dear, no, I promise! I was at a campaign mee-" I attempted to explain as she walked out of the room, down the stairs, and out the front door.

No use. I'm not sure why I continue trying with her. Maybe Barcelona was right — I need someone to give me a LaQuinta Day each morning, I thought to myself as I got ready for the inevitably long day. *I just hope today doesn't go down like yesterday did. I guess I should give Bartosz a call to let him know I'm alive and the campaign is still on.*

I looked down at my phone to four missed calls and voicemails from a +48 number. I was confused for a second until I remembered that I never saved Bartosz' Polish number into my contact list. I did so before giving him a call back.

"CONNOR, thankfully you're okay and got back to me. I have updat-"

"Bartosz, sit down and listen. We need to have a heart-to-heart about this campaign," I said with immense magnitude.

"Oh, did you already hear?" he attempted to say.

"Look, I know you were pretty busy studying all yesterday, so you probably don't recall the election events that went down."

"You're correct, but after reading the email we all received this morning, Montgomery filled me i-"

"So I'll update you on the events before we discuss anything serious. As you know, we were hacked. And so were all the other candidates. That part's not a surprised to you. What is a surprise are the pieces of the puzzle I've collected from yesterday's events that might show us who exactly hired the hacker. Chalmers Topaz – Barcelona LaQuinta's Godfather, and richest man in town – showed up unannounced and uninvited to our campaign benefit kickoff at FUCC. This is suspicious because his Goddaughter is technically still married to Jack Lozenge, one of our opponents. I attempted to accuse Jack of the hacking after Montgomery O'Donnell's disqualification, and of wanting the position of City Comptroller in order to benefit his 3-ring binder company PHUC, but it didn't get me far. Furthermore, Barcelona secretly told me yesterday that Chalmers wants Jack to win in order to secure an international multi-million dollar LaQuinta Airport Motel branded 3-ring binder deal. However, Barcelona isn't on board with any of it. Her and Jack are separated, and she's actually planning on funding Gina Cankersore's campaign to ensure Jack's defeat in the case that I become disqualified."

"Yes, Connor, as I said Montgomery

already updated me on all of that. But how is any of this information going to help with the email we were sent by K-"

"I know, Bartosz, it's a lot to take in. Feel free to take a minute to digest it and work with me on our best angles. I mean, I'm sure it'll be smooth sailing for a little bit – I have no clue how today can top yesterday!" I said, still having not heard a single word he said.

"All right, I'll just come out and say it: CONNOR, EVERYONE IN THE TOWN RECEIVED AN EMAIL FROM KIM. THE ELECTION COMMITTEE NEEDS US DOWN AT THE TOWN RHOMBUS BY 12:30 PM. IT SEEMS TODAY COULD VERY WELL END UP LIKE YESTERDAY," he screamed as if his life depended on it.

"Geesh, Bartosz, calm down. Why didn't you just say that at the beginning?"

"I-"

"Well, it's 12:05 PM now. I'll come pick you up and we'll head straight to the meeting. That should give us just enough time to make it. Be ready – I'll be there in 5 minutes," I said before I hung up and rushed out to my car.

$ $ $

On our way to the meeting, I asked Bartosz to take his phone out and send the hacker a message.

"Bartosz, take your phone out and send the hacker a message."

"Do you really think that's the best idea, Connor?" he questioned.

"Don't question me. Just do what I say," I retorted.

"I thought the Campaign Manager was supposed to consult the candidate on the best course of actions to take. You're kind of just calling all the shots, Connor."

"I didn't hire a Campaign Manager I met at a Walmart in order to be told what to do. Now just send the message," I stressed.

"Okay, whatever you say. And what would you like me to send?"

I thought for a minute. "Tell the hacker that the campaign of Connor M. Gleim has a trick up its sleeve. Tell them we hope they're in attendance at the town meeting taking place in the next 15 minutes. Then tell them they won't want to miss it!"

Bartosz typed away for a few minutes, ensuring that he used all of the correct letters and that his English was perfect. "Are there any specifics you want me to tell them? Or that you want to tell me at all? I don't know anything of this plan! Again, I'm your campaign manager!" he exclaimed.

"Okay, fine. I'll tell you, even though you'll see it in literally five minutes," I said.

"Five? You just told me to tell the hacker 15 minutes! Are you okay, Connor? I know yesterday was brutal and that you woke up unusually late, but it's only day two of the election!" Bartosz stated in a worried state.

"Yes, I'm fine. Don't be dramatic. What I mean is that we aren't on track for the town meeting right now. I have one more person to pick up. He's the surprise," I explained with an air of mystery. "So you'll be the first person aware of what's going on."

"Okay, and who is this person?" he questioned.

"His name is Colin and he's going to be

the reason this election cycle gets turned around. He'll make or break our campaign as we know it. And it's extremely important that I get him to the announcer's podium before Kim begins telling the town the news of whatever's coming."

"Colin? That's all you're going to give me? Not even a last name? Connor, this could be a bad idea," Bartosz begged.

"I don't even know his last name. Besides, what's the worst that could happen? I found him on Craigslist and told him I would pay him $5,000 to tell a personal heart-wrenching story to the whole town. And then announce his support for me," I said with a smile on my face after realizing again how brilliant that plan was.

"That sounds incredibly dumb, Connor. Does Colin's heart-wrenching story even tie into you or your campaign? Will it even be true? You're not even paying me to be your Campaign Manager for 90 whole days, yet you're giving some other kid $5,000 to say a random story you haven't even vetted and then tell the crowd to vote for you? Please don't say this is common in Amer-"

"This is common in American politics, Bartosz! I'm sorry, but your experience as a Campaign Manager and first class seat to witness one of the most important elections in the United States is much more valuable than $5,000. If it helps, I'll buy you a gift card to The Male's Shop so you can buy a professional suit that looks better than what you currently have on," I said while eyeing his wrinkly sports coat up and down. I turned my eyes back to the road and plan at hand. "Anyway, you spoke so long that we're here now."

"Connor, we aren't even in town anymore. This is the country. These people can't even vote for you."

Before I could explain anything else to him, I pulled my convertible Lexus up to a run-down house with a boarded up door and two little children playing in a dirt-soaked inflatable pool in the front yard. There was a woman smoking a cigarette in a lawn chair five feet from the children. She took one look at the car, flicked her cigarette to the grass, and immediately grabbed a shotgun that was holstered next to her.

"GIT OFF MAH LAWN," the woman screamed as she pointed the shotgun right at me and Bartosz. "I DONE TOLD YOU YUPPY BIZNESSMEN I WON'T HAVE YOU COMIN' 'ROUND HERE NO MORE. YER 3-RING BINDERS ARE SHIT 'N THEY'RE TOO EXPENSIVE ANYWAYS."

I exited my car with my arms up. "Please ma'am, put the gun down. We're not businessmen from PHUC — we're the gentlemen from Craigslist who hired someone at this residence named Colin," I explained with a slight whimper caused by the terror I felt at the sight of her loaded gun.

She turned around and stuck her head through a shattered window. "COLIN! TWO RICH GUYS ARE HERE FER YOU. THEY SAID SOMETHIN' 'BOUT SOMETHIN' CALLED CRAIGLIST. ARE YOU SNEAKIN' OFF TO THA PUBLIC LIBARY AGIN TO GET ON THOSE COMPHEWTERS? I DONE ALREADY TOLD YOU WE DON'T BELIEVE IN NO TECHNOLOLLYGY IN THIS HOUSE. IF I WANTED THA GOV'MENT TO FIND

YOU, I WOULD HAVE POPPED YOU OUT AT THA HOPSITAL 'N GOTTEN YOU A BIRTH CERTIFICATE 'N SOCIAL SECURITY NUMBA. GET YER ASS DOWN HERE NOW!"

A short, yet somehow simultaneously tall, teenage boy stumped his way down the stairs and crawled out the hole in the shattered window, being careful not to cut himself on the shards that still stuck out of the frame.

"OUCH, MAMA, MY LONG LEG GOT CUT AGIN," he yelped as his mother threw him a pile of used gauze that sat under the window. "Who did you say these guys were?"

I reached out my arm and said, "Colin! Hi, it's Connor M. Gleim for City Comptr-"

Before I could finish, Colin nervously laughed and said to his mother, "Oh, these jus' tha guys who're lookin' to buy one of our sheeps, mama. You know how animal husbandry goes – I gotta get in their car to do bizness at their offices now."

"All right, Colin, but you gotta be back by dinner. Don't nobody in this house know how to slaughter a chicken 'n cook it like you," Colin's mother said before sitting back down and yanking her cigarette out of the mouth of a goat that wondered over.

"Will do, mama. All right – c'mon guys. Let's talk animals," Colin said before getting in the back of my car.

"What the hell was that?" I interrogated as we drove away from the house that didn't seem big enough to house a farm, but apparently did anyway.

"Sorry y'all, my mama is big aginst politicians 'n the like. She don't trust nobody or nothin'. She don't like comphewters, big bizness, or tha gov'ment. She listens to a load of conspiracies. It was fer tha best that I saved y'all's asses back there," Colin explained in a way that only made us understand half of his words. I could only imagine what Bartosz was picking up on.

Colin began fiddling around with his seat belt. "Y'all real fancy like! Got a seatbelt 'n all in this here car! I haven't sawn one since I were jus' a baby."

Bartosz turned his head and whispered carefully, "Connor, are you sure this is going to work? The kid doesn't seem to know English. How is he going to give a speech to the town and then endorse you?"

"Bartosz, that *is* English. It's just what people who live out in the country sound like. If you listen carefully, he actually is saying words you know — you just have to understand how to decipher them a little bit. I'm not worried at all. The town might actually feel bad for him," I explained, making sure that Colin was still too preoccupied with figuring out how to put on a seatbelt to hear me.

"Phew, all buckled in now. Say, y'all got any water? I gets real parched 'fore speakin'. Doctor says it's cuz my long leg needs more hydration," Colin said as he propped both his legs up on the center console for us to see. "See, one leg longer than tha other! Ain't that somethin'!"

"Yeah, that's really something," Bartosz said as he began to realize how to translate Colin's dialect into proper English.

I looked at the rearview mirror to see Colin smiling out of pride in the backseat. "Colin, I need you to listen, okay? We don't have time to look at the fact that you have a slightly longer leg than the other. You'll be speaking for approximately 30 minutes on the hardship of your choice. Your goal is to get the audience to feel for you – establish a connection between their pathos and your personal heart-wrenching story. You got that?"

"Yessir!"

"Okay, now this is very important. I just need to make sure I understand what your hardship is. Walk me through it so there aren't any surprises. I know this town extremely well, and I can help you tweak some things in your speech to get them on board with voting for me," I explained as we headed towards the Town Rhombus, only 3 minutes remaining until Kim took to the podium.

"Well, this is it! This is my hardship!" Colin said as he pointed to his legs, which were still hoisted up on the center console.

Bartosz laughed, "Good one, Colin. I think I'm starting to understand the humor of you Americans."

"Ain't nothin' funny 'bout it! I gone through hard times thanks to these here legs. One's short, 'n the other… well, it's long!" Colin retorted.

"Yeah, we get that, Colin. But how exactly is that a hardship, and how are you going to connect with the audience with… *that?*" I questioned.

"Well, when I was jus' 18 months old, my mama-"

I interrupted him as I forced the car into a stop with the smash of the brakes. "Sorry, Colin, but you're going to have to save it for the audience. We're here and you have…" I looked down at my watch, "exactly one minute to rush up to that microphone and start talking before Kim announces what we're all here for."

"Now, see, I wouldn't've bin able ta do that there brake-smashing with my short leg — I woulda hadda use my long one," Colin said with a smirk on his face. "Not so simple now, is it?"

"Whatever you say," I said as I pulled Colin out of the car. "Now run up to the podium NOW."

As me and Bartosz got situated among the crowd, we saw as Colin was sort of running/hopping/skipping/dancing his way to the stage. It was clear that his hardship actually did prevent him from walking or running properly.

I pulled in to Bartosz and whispered, "Maybe this will work after all. I'm already feeling sorry for him myself!"

Bartosz rolled his eyes, shoveled his hands onto his face, and took a deep breath in and out.

Just as Kim was two steps from the microphone, Colin completed his journey and began speaking.

"Hi y'all, I'm Colin!"

Kim was shocked and immediately walked back to the other side of the stage.

"And I'm gun tell y'all somethin' that may jus' change yer minds about who to vote fer in this here 'lection." There was a long pause as Colin lifted up his mud-stained jeans and pulled out a stack of paper notecards that were being contained by his long johns. "Y'all know any good speaker gotta have his cards prepared," he said with a laugh at the end.

The crowd laughed with him, surprisingly. *Hmm, I guess he does have a sense of likability with the general public*, I thought to myself.

Bartosz leaned over to me and whispered,

"Connor, I don't want to rain on your parade, but look at the notecards he's holding up."

I looked up and noticed that Colin was holding a stack of PHUC branded notecards. *SHIT! This is free publicity for Jack Lozenge's 3-ring binder company!* "I don't think anyone will notice. Besides, it's the story and endorsement that counts," I whispered back to Bartosz.

Colin continued. "Y'all might've noticed I was walkin' up here funny 'n all. Well that's becuz one-ah my legs is long'r than tha other!"

The crowd *awww*'d and hung on every word Colin said. I was blown away. Personally, me and Bartosz didn't see the appeal of his story. But apparently everyone else did! We kept exchanging glances with each other like *Is this for real?* and *How is he doing so well giving a speech about having one leg that just happens to be slightly longer than the other?* It was completely unbelievable. I didn't expect the speech to turn out this well!

"And then when I was jus' six-years-old, I couldn't walk in a straight line wit' tha rest uv tha first graders! The teachers kept gettin' onta me fer gettin' outta line!"

He was about halfway through his 30-minute speech and the crowd was already crying. Bartosz and I looked around as we saw streams of tears falling off the faces of almost everyone in the crowd. I looked to the other side of the stage to see Kim and the entire election committee hugging each other and bawling.

"But tha hardest part came when I qual'fied fer free leg reduction surgery! That's when they make one-ah yer legs shorter so that both legs match up. Well... les jus' say they made tha long leg a lil' TOO short! Now my short leg is my long leg, and my long leg is my short leg! Canya belee dat!"

The crowd was hysterical at this point. Most of the audience members were calling their loved ones. A camera crew was called and set up just in front of the stage to televise the speech to the nation. Colin was trending on Twitter! I couldn't be more surprised and proud of how this was going. I leaned over to Bartosz, "Told you this was a smart move."

"I cannot believe that this is what Americans consider inspirational and news-worthy..." Bartosz said in disbelief before we turned our eyes back to Colin to hear the finale of his speech.

"'N that's why you shud vote for Connor M. Gleim as yer next City Comptroller!" Colin said as the crowd jumped up and cheered.

As Colin began to crowd-surf, Bartosz nudged me and showed me a message our campaign account received from the hacker. It said, "That was the most inspirational speech I've ever heard. It only makes my heart hurt for what's about to happen next. If only I had heard Colin's story a couple hours ago…"

"What do you think they mean by that?" I asked Bartosz as my expression turned from excitement to worriment.

"I don't know, but I have a feeling it means that what Kim is about to say into that microphone is about our campaign."

I watched as Kim wiped the tears from her eyes, hugged Colin, and stepped up to the podium.

"Thank you all for being here this afternoon. While we were supposed to announce our news 30 minutes ago, I am more than happy that we were intercepted by the wonderful young man known as Colin.

Colin, I think I speak for all 20,000 of us here tonight when I say that you have overcome *so* much, and that we hope you continue inspiring the world with your story of one leg being slightly longer than the other."

The crowd applauded and braced themselves for the shift of emotions they were about to experience.

Kim continued. "Now, I know we're all still taken aback from the events of yesterday. Collectively disqualifying a candidate is never easy. I understand that. Unfortunately… the election committee received another tip that could lead to the disqualification of another candidate."

Everyone gasped and switched their mindset from inspired to panicked.

"Can I have each of the remaining candidates up on the stage, please. Connor Gleim, Jack Lozenge, and Gina Candyshop."

We all headed to the stage with a familiar feeling: dread. On stage, I looked out at the crowd, gulping as they stared back. Suddenly my eye caught a flash in the crowd. Barcelona's diamond bracelet caught the light and was reflecting a beam straight at my face.

I looked at her longingly, taking the reflection as a sign of fate. *Maybe I should be with her*, I thought to myself. Just as I finished that thought, I saw Misty – my wife – standing right next to my mistress. In that moment, I was immediately conflicted on what to do. Unfortunately – or maybe fortunately – that choice would be made for me just seconds later.

"Connor Gleim! Why don't you tell the town why we're here today?" Kim announced.

My heart sunk. I saw Misty's angry face next to Barcelona's happy one. It was clear they knew what I was about to say. I shifted my gaze to Bartosz, who donned both a surprised expression and a disappointed one. He had no clue what I was about to admit because I told him there was nothing to hide. I lied to him, and now he was about to be the Campaign Manager of a disgraced candidate. I saw Montgomery in the crowd, urging me to go on and tell the crowd my secret, but in a way that would make them keep me as a candidate. I saw the eyes of the town residents waiting for me to say something, anything.

"I'm not a man of many words, so I'll just

come out and say it. I've committed adultery against my wife, Misty Gleim. I've been seeing Barcelona LaQuinta, in a romantic and sexual nature, for the past year. Forgive me – it's what Colin would want," I said before I gripped my hands and closed my eyes, waiting for objects to be thrown at me just like Montgomery experienced during his disqualification.

To my surprise, nothing happened. I waited a good five seconds and then opened my eyes to find everyone standing in the same spot. Don't get me wrong, they looked disappointed, but there wasn't the huge uproar I expected.

If anything, it appeared I was the person most angry at myself. "C'mon! Aren't you going to throw things at me? Call me names? Start a town fight? Disqualify me, even?"

Some man yelled, "Not really. Every guy in this town has been with Barcelona LaQuinta. Our wives have kind of gotten used to us committing adultery by now!"

Then some women yelled, "Yeah, and a couple of us women have even gone to town once or twice with Barcelona. I'm pretty sure every one of us has had our share. You're not special!"

While it was a relief to hear the town wasn't mad, I made sure to glance over to the one person whose opinion mattered. Misty was simultaneously furious and sobbing. She ran out of the crowd, and before I could run after her, Kim laid down the verdict.

"Well, it seems you've been saved, Connor. The town has chosen not to disqualify you. I don't know if it was the influence of Colin or if you just picked the right woman to commit adultery with, but your campaign lives to see another day," Kim said as she shook my hand and welcomed me back to where the other candidates were standing.

I turned to see where Misty had run off to, but she was nowhere to be found. I felt terrible. On one hand, I was extremely happy that I could continue campaigning and that my only secret in life was off my chest. On the other hand, I had destroyed my marriage, and possibly my relationship with my daughter, Marge.

Before I knew it, Barcelona jumped up on stage and pulled me back to the podium. She put her mouth up to the microphone – getting a little lipstick on it – and said, "Ladies and gentlemen, I am honored to announce my place as the new First Lady to the campaign of Connor M. Gleim!"

CHAPTER 5
ENRON: THE MUSICAL

I want to take a break from my true life story to workshop the musical screenplay I've been writing for the past four years. It's called <u>Enron: The Musical</u>, and it's about the 2001 financial scandal and series of fraud committed by the American energy and services company known as Enron.

Enron was started by this guy named Kenneth Lay and largely operated by another guy named Jeffrey Skilling. Lay fortunately died due to a heart attack I hope is connected to the guilt he felt for defrauding millions of people, and Skilling is unfortunately still alive. There's also this guy named Andrew Fastow, but I always forget he exists (which he shouldn't).

Anyway, they were in the natural gas and, ultimately, energy business down in Houston, Texas – as one does. For a couple of years, their stock prices were the highest on the market, thanks to the executives selling their stocks during massive losses (hello, insider trading) while simultaneously telling their investors, their employees, and the general public that they should 100% continue buying stocks (hello, conspiracy). In essence, this overvalued their stocks, leaving Journalists and Economists wondering exactly how Enron was making that much money. They're also responsible for the infamous 2000-2001 California Energy Crisis, in which Enron colluded with energy suppliers to purposefully black-out the whole state in order to institute "premium" power prices that were up to 20x higher than normal. And let's not forget that while both of these situations – and many more – were happening, the Bush administration made sure Enron and its need to defraud the world were heard on Capitol Hill.

There is a LOT more to this story – what I

provided is about 25%. So I suggest you read the Wikipedia page or something. But this isn't about them! This is about me and my musical adaptation! Let's get right into it:

INT — OFFICE — DAY

Enron Executives are drinking scotch on the 50th floor of the 1400 Smith Street skyscraper, also known as the Enron Complex.

KENNETH LAY
Jeffrey Skilling, my right hand man, Enron has been doing really well for the past decade. Do you think we should ruin it by introducing fraud and illegal activities into our business model?

JEFFREY SKILLING
Kenneth Lay, my boss and owner of this company we call Enron, I see you have asked me a question. Let me analyze that,

as a Chief Operations Officer often does. Analyzation 100% complete! Yes, I do believe my algorithm has detected that scamming the world out of billions will increase our personal revenues significantly.

ANDREW FASTOW
My name is Andrew Fastow and I have the accountants for the job. We can conceal Enron's massive losses through shell companies I've created. My wife also works here.

LEA FASTOW
I am his wife.

ALL FOUR IN UNISON
Let's just publish Enron's Code of Ethics real quick so no one suspects anything.

**INSERT HIP-HOP MUSICAL NUMBER WHERE THE CHARACTERS SING AND RAP ALL 65 PAGES OF THE ENRON 'CODE OF ETHICS'

DOCUMENT**

Enters Sherron Watkins

SHERRON WATKINS
What is going on here!? Scandal is afoot! I didn't agree to be a Vice President at Enron so that we could lie to everyone! I'm about to blow that whistle. I warned you, Kenneth Lay!

Sherron calls the government.

SHERRON WATKINS
Hello, government. Yes, my name is Sherron Watkins, future *Time* Person Of The Year, and I am here to whistleblow on my employer Enron. There are irregularities in the financial reports. Yes, I can hold.

While on hold, Sherron sings a ballad about the importance of doing the right thing.

THE GOVERNMENT
Good news, Sherron. Enron is done for, and all of the people at the beginning of this musical are in prison now. Hooray!

That's pretty much it. Did you like it? I'm not worried about the length because the 65-page 'Enron Code of Ethics' musical number should last a good two hours. It has a sort of Hamilton vibe to it, huh?

If you have any suggestions on how to make the musical stronger, feel free to email me at EnronTheMusical@gmail.com.

CHAPTER 6
TWO CENTS

The next 81 days were pretty tame compared to the first two days of the campaign, but boy were they busy! Here's a detailed update about all of us:

$ <u>Connor M. Gleim & Barcelona LaQuinta</u> After being outed as an adulterer, I decided to do right by the town and be the politician they wanted and deserved. I wore a scarlet letter 'A' across my chest at all times, I divorced Misty and started seeing Barcelona as my Campaign First Lady, and I began volunteering for all sorts of causes around town. I donated to the homeless, I helped orphans ride motorcycles, and I even taught financial literacy to dogs at the animal shelter. I basically did everything I could to restructure my reputation in a town that could have easily disqualified me. And Barcelona was right there the entire time. In fact, she was a better source of reputation management for my campaign. She was seen around town as an 'Evita' type figure, mainly because she distributed funding by throwing dollar bills out of train windows as it drove by the common townspeople. She also made her catchphrase a source of immense hope for the poor population. Each time they heard "Have a LaQuinta Day!" they knew they had to vote for me. And of course, Barcelona pulled her funding out of Gina Candlestick's campaign. Without the threat of disqualification, me and Barcelona no longer needed to have a contingency plan.

$ Misty & Margaret Gleim

After our divorce, Misty began seeing my opponent, Jack Lozenge. I know she only did it to get back at me, but I didn't mind because I guess we were even considering I was with Jack's estranged wife. She played her cards right because now she had two candidates in the race that would keep Marge's future school – FUKK – open and potentially save her favorite brunch place: FUC. Speaking of Margaret, she was excelling in her summer FUKK camp. She was on track to receive the title of Star-FUKR: Star Future University Kindergartener Reward. Despite her parents' divorce and the new love interests we brought into her life, Marge was doing better than ever.

$ Jack Lozenge & Chalmers Topaz

The town didn't take too kindly to Jack and Misty getting together after our divorce. They almost disqualified Jack with the reason stating "Pettiness." Apparently this town takes less kindly to Pettiness than Adultery, surprisingly. Regardless, he was able to continue running his campaign, but fell several points in the polls. While I was rising in the polls due to my humanitarian efforts and likable Campaign First Lady, Jack was slipping hard. He was seen as the clear front-runner for about a month after Montgomery was disqualified, but now we were neck-and-neck. Now, just ahead of the Election Debate between the three remaining candidates, Jack's poll numbers were mere decimal points ahead of mine. Also contributing to his downfall in the polls was PC Newsick Journalist Charlie Exséecks breaking the news that Jack may be running for City Comptroller solely to revive his 3-ring binder company: PHUC. While this news was not shocking to me, the town began to speculate and run with conspiracy theories. Chalmers Topaz, too, began to make headlines not only as Jack Lozenge's top funder, but also as PHUC's top stakeholder. After

Charlie Exséecks connected those dots and theorized that Chalmers could be colluding and engaging in insider trading with Jack in order to remain the richest man in town, Chalmers began keeping a very close eye on all of the campaigns and keeping a low profile. He also cleaned up his fraudulent activities within the election, which included hiring...

$ The Hacker

After the Charli Exséecks story broke, the campaign hacker reached out to me and Bartosz to explain everything. They neglected to provide their name out of fear that they could be prosecuted, but they wanted to make up for everything they did to us. They promised to admit everything they knew if we promised not to leak it to the other campaigns or Kim. Their primary motivation for this promise was the determination that they could help our campaign in ways that would far exceed the damage Jack's campaign would take by leaking the truth. Essentially, Jack's campaign *was* behind hiring the hacker, just as I suspected. However, there was one piece of key information I wasn't expecting: Chalmers was actually the person who hired the hacker on behalf of Jack's team – and Jack had no knowledge of what was going on. In order to cover up traces of this, Chalmers had the hacker target Jack, as well. Jack's fear of leaked information leading to a disqualification was genuine, but Chalmers knew it would truly never happen. The hacker admitted Chalmers had no other dirt on me that wasn't already public (i.e. the affair). The hacker stated they chose to tell my campaign all of this and support me because of us being "the only campaign with a chance of beating Jack Lozenge."

$ Bartosz Wiśniewski & Rebecca

To supplement his experience in the United States, Bartosz got a second summer internship as Montgomery's personal assistant and caretaker. His primary duty consisted of tending to Montgomery's papercuts, as Montgomery was still receiving public backlash and having his own ghostwritten *auto*biography thrown at him everywhere he went in town. Fortunately, this – coupled with his Health Science summer course – lead Bartosz to find his passion in Medicine. He decided to switch majors from Political Science to Public Health and, thus, transfer from Politics & Humanities Undergraduate College (PHUC) to Public Health Undergraduate College (PHUC), the leading Pre-Med college in town. After transferring, he met Rebecca, a Medical Tech Graphic Design student who offered to create and provide the graphic standards and brand guidelines for my campaign accounts. She became a valuable member of the Connor M. Gleim campaign! And she couldn't have come at a better time – when we desperately needed graphics for the

Election Debate!

$ <u>Gina Canyon</u>

$ <u>Colin</u>

Colin was able to get cosmetic surgery that re-shortened his long leg, and re-longened his short leg. He is now back to his old self, before the first doctor botched his initial operation!

CHAPTER 7
BET YOUR BOTTOM DOLLAR

The day arrived. The City Comptroller Election Debate largely determines who's going to do well during the final stretch of the election cycle. Because there hadn't been one in over 20 years, it made the pressure even more extreme.

Jack, Gina, and I all looked at the crowd from behind the curtain at the back of the stage. It appeared that, yet again, all 20,000 residents of the town were in attendance. Not only that, but the local news station – PC Newsick – set up their cameras all around the Town Rhombus, and someone got Kim to agree to let Journalist Charlie Exséecks be the host of the event. By extension, right next to her was Agey Kook, creator of PC Newsick and top Reporter. Not only would these two be the hosts and moderators of the debate, they would be televising it to the entire nation. It seemed our scandal-ridden election made its way as entertainment to the other states!

"Good luck everybody," I said to the other two candidates and their campaign team members as they mic'd us up and prepared us for the stage.

"I don't need luck – I'm still at the top of the polls, after all," Jack smirked while bossing his copious amount of team members around to do things from ironing his shirt to polishing his shoes.

"Thanks Connor, good lu-" Gina attempted to say before Kim interrupted her by announcing the rules of the first debate to the crowd.

"As you all know, it has been a bumpy ride to get here. We started with four candidates for the position of City Comptroller. One has been disqualified, two have faced and survived disqualification, and the final one is barely making high enough poll numbers to constitute being here. Regardless of scandals, campaign leaks, and countless reputation face-lifts, we are finally commencing our City Comptroller Election Debate tonight!

"The candidates are right behind this curtain," Kim stated as she waved her hand behind her in the curtain's direction. "I will now request that they come out one at a time.

"Jack Lozenge! You are the current front-runner, albeit only decimal points ahead of your strongest opponent. You have survived scandals consisting of conspiracies, fraudulent behavior, and insider trading. Quite frankly, I'm surprised the town hasn't actually disqualified you yet, but that may speak volumes to how effective you could be while in office. Please step up to your podium at the right-hand side of front-stage!"

Jack Lozenge had two of his campaign assistants hold open the curtain in an eloquent manner as he stepped out onto the stage in the most expensive and exquisite suit that money could buy. He confidently waved to the crowd before walking to the front of the stage to pick up a baby that a woman was holding up in the VIP section. He gave the baby a kiss on the forehead and the crowd cheered.

Kim continued. "Connor M. Gleim! You are basically neck-and-neck with Jack Lozenge for the spot of our next City Comptroller. However, your track record projects you could easily defeat him if you continue the steam your campaign is getting from our townspeople. You are popular among the lower-socioeconomic class, but will that be enough for you to be effective in office? Your only scandal includes committing adultery, which you somehow turned from a negative to a positive in the eyes of your constituents. Please step up to your podium at the left-hand side of front-stage!"

I pulled back the curtain and stepped out onto the stage with a huge applause and roar from the crowd. It was clear that my political momentum meant something to the townspeople. I gave a wave to the audience and blew a kiss to Barcelona, which made the crowd go even more wild. I shook Jack's hand and then headed to my podium right next to his at the front of the stage.

"And finally, Gina Cannibal! Your poll numbers barely allowed you to be here today.

In fact, the Election Committee may actually change the rules to raise the poll count required to be here because there is no way in hell you're going to win!" Kim said as the crowd laughed. "Either way, you have conducted a clean campaign with absolutely no scandals or excitement. At one point you had the heiress of an airport motel chain funding you, but you quickly lost that support. You now have zero funders, and you have yet to find a campaign manager with only a week left in the election. All I can say is, good luck! Please step up to your podium at the back of the stage!"

Gina came out struggling to pull back the curtain. She tripped over the curtain tassels and made her short way to the podium in what looked like a crawl-limp hybrid. It didn't take her much time at all to arrive at her podium, as it was pretty far back on the stage – almost half of it being covered by the curtain itself. She waved to the audience as they sat in silence. She attempted to say, "My last name is actually Cany-"

"All right! I'll hand the reigns over to our humble moderators: Charlie Exséecks and

Agey Kook of PC Newsick! Let's give them a big round of applause before we get started tonight!"

The crowd stood up and clapped before getting settled back into their seats for the next two hours. Meanwhile, Charlie and Agey settled at the moderators' table, got their debate questions prepared, and turned on a huge screen to the left of the stage. People *wow*'d at its sheer size and resolution.

"All right, everybody! Put your hands up!" yelled Charlie. "Do you see yourself on the jumbotron? That will be used to spotlight those of you who are having the most fun tonight! Put 'em up, put 'em up! Party!" she exclaimed into her microphone as the crowd began to use their arms to plead for the jumbotron's attention.

Agey placed his mouth near the microphone. "As you all know, this debate is being broadcasted – visually and audibly – to the entire nation, so you have the opportunity of being seen on national television! Isn't that exciting?"

I glanced over to Bartosz, who was shaking his head incredulously. He caught my gaze and mouthed, "Why?" which made me chuckle a little bit. He still wasn't used to how we do thing in the states.

"All right, now let's get started!" Charlie stated. "First question: What is the highest priority on your platform, or what is your first order of business when you become City Comptroller? You may answer one or both questions — and we understand if your answer is the same for both."

Remember, Connor, let Jack answer first as many times as possible, analyze his answers as much as possible, and then answer based on how you feel the town reacted to Jack's answer, I thought to myself. I knew Jack would be the type of self-centered candidate to dominate the debate by attempting to answer first every single time. And just like clockwork…

"I'll answer first," Jack announced into his microphone. "My first order of business as City Comptroller will be the same as my campaign's highest priority: Ensure the city isn't Cloud-dependent on their financial *paper*work and documentation. We're going on 10 years now as a digital-only city, ever since O'Donnell's Consulting Firm convinced Gina

Gorge to move from physical documentation backup to digital, Cloud-based backup. This makes our city more susceptible to data loss and hacking!"

Oh, hacking! That's real rich coming from Jack Lozenge, I thought at my podium while I watched as the audience reacted to his answer and demeanor.

Agey nodded his head and then asked, "And what would you say to skeptics of your campaign who believe that the only reason you want to move back to physical financial paperwork and documentation is to increase the revenue of your 3-ring binder company, which includes selling reams of paper?"

Everyone in the audience was on the edge of their seats.

"So what? That's not illegal… is it?" Jack answered.

Just as expected, the audience reacted with disappointment. Now was my time to pounce.

I leaned into my microphone. "Now before you continue this line of questioning, I do want to say that I agree somewhat with Jack's sentiment. As City Comptroller, one of my first orders of business would be to classify different types of financial paperwork and documentation. While I agree with the majority of city opinion that digital storage is the most ethical and sensible way to deal with business documentation, I also believe that there are just certain documents that are too valuable to leave up in the Cloud. As City Comptroller, I would institute a document caste system, in which only the important of important financial paperwork and documents would be exempt from digitization and, thus, allowed to be restored in their physical form," I announced with confidence and force.

The crowd cheered. It was clear that they enjoyed that I reiterated their majority opinion, and that I was humble enough to reach a level of agreeance with an opponent — especially such an unlikable one.

"Here's what I would do if I wo-" Gina attempted before being cut off by Charlie and Agey.

"Candidates, many people from all around the nation are watching right now. You've kicked up national attention through the variety of unprecedented scandals experienced through just 83 days. Are there any scandals the U.S. public can expect from you if you win City Comptroller, or will you focus solely on doing your job?"

Per usual, Jack jumped at the chance to speak first, clearly not learning his lesson to think before he speaks. "Hey America, I want to thank you for supporting our little town. If it's a scandal you want, it's a scandal you'll get! As long as it keeps us on the map and get my 3-ring binders in your home, I will commit it! Vote Jack Lozenge as City Comptroller!"

Dear God, did he forget that it's not America's vote he's vying for? He needs to appeal to the residents of our city if he wants to win! I thought to myself incredulously.

The crowd looked extremely annoyed at Jack at this point. Some people had even taken off their "Avenge Lozenge" t-shirt – a marketing move by Jack's campaign when he was slipping in the polls.

"Jack, I'm not sure our residents want the next City Comptroller to make a mockery out of the position and the our town," I said with a wink to the audience. "There are ample other ways to generate publicity that doesn't include fraud, collusion, and sin. As City

Comptroller, I will vow to never commit another scandal again – instead choosing to sign a contract with Netflix for an 8-part series about what it means to be a City Comptroller in the town known for the position!"

The crowd went wild. They admired my resourcefulness to continue generating hype for the city, while ensuring more scandals aren't introduced.

"Hey! I can do that too. Maybe I'll get Netflix to make a series about my paper mill company and all of the wacky employees I house!" Jack blurted.

"I'm sorry, Jack, it is not your turn to answer," Charlie said with a stern face. "And anyway, 'The Office' already exists. Now on to our next question."

Gina hurried her face towards her microphone. "Wait! I didn't even get to answe-"

"Candidates, what state do you believe the financial health of our city is in currently, and why? What would you do to improve our financial health?"

To spare you the whole debate, I'll just say

that it was a clear win for me. PC Newsick Journalist Charlie Exséecks and Reporter Agey Kook gave my performance and delivery a 10/10, with emphasis on having the most potential to be a successful City Comptroller. Jack Lozenge was rated a 7.5/10, with the reason being that he seemed like an opportunist who was only in the race for the possibilities it would provide him and his company PHUC. Gina Cancelation wasn't rated and, instead, was given a consolation prize and a ribbon that said, "At Least She Was Here."

This debate win solidified me as the frontrunner of the election and secured my campaign with grassroots funding from around the nation. I immediately began trending on twitter concluding the debate, and my team celebrated by heading to Patty's Home Plate.

As we were heading out, I saw Misty screaming at Jack from a distance. I completely understood what that felt like, and while I was glad to be done with situations like that, I felt for the guy. When she stormed off, I went up to Jack.

"Hey Jack, good game up there. I hope I didn't seem too harsh to you near the end."

"It's all good, Connor. I'm really not worried. I still have a card or two up my sleeve."

"I'm glad you're not giving up that easily. Me and my team are headed to Patty's to celebrate, so I can't chat long. But I look forward to the rest of the election cycle!" I said before heading towards Barcelona, Montgomery, Bartosz, and Rebecca.

As I was walking away, I heard Jack emit a maniacal laugh. It spooked me a little, but I tried not to give it too much thought. *I sure hope that isn't related to the cards he has yet to play...*

CHAPTER 8
GRAVY TRAIN

While me and my campaign team were amending our campaign platform and issues based on how the audience reacted, we heard the hustle and bustle of a big crowd enter through the diner door.

"You know, even though you didn't win the debate tonight, Jack, you were the man! The town would be stupid not to elect you next week!" we heard a familiar voice say. *Chalmers*, I immediately thought to myself.

Barcelona, Montgomery, Bartosz, Rebecca, and I all turned around to see Jack Lozenge and his campaign minions bossing a server around and demanding a seat at the booth closest to us. They made their way closer to us as our table began gossiping amongst each other regarding a mysterious campaign supporter that we didn't recognize.

The rather old gentlemen behind Jack was dressed from head to toe in professional attire that seemed only available in the 1940s. He walked with a cane and had a monocle hanging from his neck. I wasn't sure if he was paying homage to the golden age of diners, or if he was just cut from a different time period.

Suddenly my eyes grew big as I realized exactly who that man was. I turned to the others and gasped, "That's Elias Loejzunjn!"

"Connor, that doesn't really explain much," retorted Bartosz.

"He's Jack's grandfather, most famous for inventing the medicated Throat Lozenge. His last name sounds exactly like Jack's, but it's spelled differently in order to pay respect to his family's original spelling before it was anglicized on Ellis Island in 1892. Jack convinced him to change the name of his medical product from 'Throat Loejzunjn' to 'Throat Lozenge' in a marketing attempt to popularize the product in the 1990s. While it worked, Elias never forgave Jack for allowing him to go against their family history. They haven't spoken since. I had a hunch Elias might come back into Jack's life in order to help him win, though. No doubt, there's another scandal brewing."

Just as I finished explaining who Elias was to my team, Jack's team walked up and sat down at the booth next to us, one by one – Jack, Misty, Chalmers, and Elias.

"Great debate up there tonight!" I attempted to say to the opponent group before they rolled their eyes.

Misty shot her eyes towards our booth and said, "Barcelona, I'm surprised you didn't try to have sex with Agey Kook while he was moderating tonight!"

"Ha ha, Misty! I've already had sex with Agey and it wasn't that good," Barcelona shot back.

"Oh hey, Montgomery!" Chalmers began. "Nice bandages. You piggy-backing off of another campaign since yours didn't work out? Do you think he's going to make you Vice City Comptroller or something? Go back to consulting!"

Montgomery looked up from watching

Bartosz applying ointment to his papercuts. "Joke's on you, Chalmers – I don't even know what a City Comptroller does. I was just running for the hell of it, and now I'm supporting the only candidate that gives a shit about this town!"

Jack looked straight into my eyes. "And Connor... you think you did so well tonight? You may slip ahead in the polls tomorrow, but I'm still out-funding you by millions, and soon to be billions. Let me introduce you to my little frien- er, Grandfather: Elias Loejzunjn."

"You're too late, Jack. I *already* explained who Elias is to the reader!" I said.

Suddenly a food fight broke out between our groups. Jack and I began fighting, Barcelona and Misty started pulling each other's hair out, and Chalmers and Montgomery pulled out their financial spreadsheets to compare who was the better businessman.

In the meantime, Bartosz and Rebecca walked over to Elias and began to chat with him.

"Connor did a pretty poor job of

describing you earlier," Bartosz said. "Since us three are the only sane ones at this diner apparently, Rebecca and I thought it would be nice to just chat."

Elias smiled. "Oh, that's nice. To be honest, I thought it might be a mistake to come here tonight. I wanted to secretly fund Jack's campaign, but he thought it would be best to show me off to his opponent, as if I'm his dick or something!"

That made Bartosz and Rebecca chuckle. "Did you really create the modern Throat Lozenge?" Rebecca asked.

"Sure did! Want some?" Elias asked as he pulled open his antiquated sports coat and showed off hundreds of individual lozenges that were all different flavors.

"Wow!" they exclaimed. "I know we're not supposed to take candy from strangers, but no one ever said anything about Throat Lozenges!" They each began to pick off a couple different lozenges, which were clearly individually licked by Elias and just stuck to the fabric of his coat.

While Bartosz was sucking on a cherry-kiwi flavored lozenge, he told Elias about his and Rebecca's dreams of attending medical school at RowanSOM in New Jersey. Rebecca then went on to talk about how inspiring it was to meet the creator of a medical miracle.

"RowanSOM, you say?" Elias asked. "You know, I grew up in New Jersey. When my parents immigrated here in 1892, they couldn't stand the city. They opted for New Jersey instead. My whole life is there. In 1976, after I created the modern Throat Lozenge and contributed much to the medical community, I was asked to sit on a committee created by the New Jersey State Legislature. Our goal was to create an impeccable medical school for the future generations to learn from. That higher education institution became known as RowanSOM," Elias explained with a grin on his face.

They noticed that the group fight was dying down and it looked like Jack was about to leave.

Elias turned back to Bartosz and Rebecca. "Say, here's my business card. You two give me a call when this whole campaign chaos is over. Both of you are too smart to be tangled up in this mess."

They began to thank him before the doors of the diner swung open. Every member of both campaign groups turned around to see Kim, Charlie, and Agey walking in and demanding to sit next to mine and Jack's booths.

"There better not be any collusion going on here! You know the candidates and their teams are not to meet each other off the record during election time!" Kim screamed as the server was seating them at a booth right in front of us.

Almost in unison, me and Jack proclaimed, "What does it matter, Kim? We're the only two candidates left in the election!"

Suddenly we heard a cough from behind our booths. Everyone turned around to see Gina Candelabra sitting alone. The state of her food suggested that she had been there the entire time, if not longer. "I'm still in the race!" Gina screamed.

Everyone began to whisper amongst their respective groups about how she got there.

Suddenly Jack stood up and slammed a metal spoon against his glass of milk. "I guess now is as good a time as any to make an official campaign announcement, considering all the candidates and election officials are in this diner tonight. I am proud to announce that my grandfather – Elias Loejzunjn – is joining my campaign as a funding source! I look forward to showing the residents of our city exactly how to properly handle financial resources!"

$ $ $

Throughout the final campaign week, Jack Lozenge began to understand what it's like to make promises to too many funders. While Chalmers was still putting immense pressure on Jack to use campaign resources to promote his 3-ring binder company, Elias started using Jack as a way to spread his Throat Lozenge propaganda around the town.

Jack assumed that he would be able to use the extra funding to repair his reputation and come across as more genuine to the residents after his hellish debate performance. Instead, Chalmers and Elias forced him and his campaign team to become walking advertisements, going door-to-door pushing 3-ring binders and Throat Lozenges. In order to keep his funding, Jack was required to wear a Throat Lozenge™ t-shirt 24/7 (even while not campaigning) and deliver a 3-ring binder filled to the brim with information about the benefits of using 3-ring binders to every resident.

By the end of the official election cycle, Jack Lozenge knew he had botched his campaign, worse than that doctor botched Colin's leg shortening surgery. However, he still had enough funding to influence the polls. By the time Election Night rolled around, me and Jack were neck-and-neck — decimal point to decimal point — on the polls…

CHAPTER 9
DAYLIGHT ROBBERY

Flashing lights. That's all I saw as the crowd of 20,000 people grew more and more silent in anticipation, staring right back at me and the few others on the stage. They had a good reason to be hanging on every heartbeat we sounded, for this was the night. Election Night. And not just any election night – the City Comptroller Election Night.

All eyes were on me – Connor Gleim – and my opponent Jack Lozenge. It was a neck-and-neck race, anybody's game. We were tied in the polls, we had an equal amount of scandals throughout the race, and we both had the grit it took to become a politician – more importantly, a Comptroller. Oh! And

Gina was there. However, Gina did not matter in the City Comptroller race against me and Jack.

After 20 years, Gina finally had an opponent in the City Comptroller race. Two, at that. And the election night came down to either me, the beloved Connor Gleim whom the city had admiration for (with much thanks to the new wife, Barcelona), or Jack Lozenge. With as many flashing lights as there were that night, you'd think that the winner of the race was Electromagnetic Radiation. But just as we were blinded by the rays, and deafened by the silence of the crowd awaiting voting results, Kim began to speak.

"Hello everyone. As the designated elections announcer, I want to remind you all how hard we have been working that poll. You'll remember that – in an attempt to make the voting process a little more lively – we constructed flash mob events at all polling locations across the city. And boy did we dance those polls. I want to thank all of you, especially the ones who donated by tossing dollar bills at our dancers and screaming, 'Get it, shawty.' We're not entirely sure what you meant, but your contributions made this election night possible.

"And without further ado, I will open this envelope and announce the winner of our city's next Comptroller.

"And the winner is…

Jack Lozenge!

I couldn't believe what I had just heard. Jack Lozenge? The guy who wasn't sorry for his scandals, committed insider trading with rich people to help their bank accounts, had a terrible campaign platform that lost him the debate, and spent the final week of campaigning just giving out Throat Lozenges and 3-ring binders door-to-door? That guy won?

I burrowed my hands into my face while Jack began to crowd surf over the audience.

Meanwhile, I caught a glimpse of Gina sneaking behind the curtain and changing into a disguise that included only a fake mustache and a trench coat.

She ran back out to the stage and exclaimed, "Connor M. Gleim and Jack Lozenge colluded with the Elections Committee to keep Gina Canyon from winning by removing her name from the ballot!"

I leaned into my microphone and stated, "That's not even possible because I forgot you were running, Gina. And yes, I know it's you because you're the only person who remembers how to say your own last name correctly."

Kim walked back up to her podium and announced, "I concur. I just consulted with the Elections Committee and we, too, forgot Gina was running. We officially apologize for forgetting to add Gina Carnival's name on the ballot. As a courtesy, we would like any audience member to raise their hand if they would have voted for Gina as the next City Comptroller."

The crowd was silent, instead deciding to

continue cheering for Jack.

$ $ $

It was a week after my loss and I was walking around FUC Park – Frank Ufford City Park – thinking about all of the positive memories the campaign trail afforded me. I grew to love and respect Bartosz, Barcelona, Montgomery, Rebecca, and even the social media hacker. I couldn't have asked for a better team. I was able to get out of my dying marriage and into a new one with Barcelona. I guess the real election was the friends I made along the way.

I began to grow relief for not winning, actually. Just as I started to smile for the first time in a week, a figure darted out of the bushes to my left.

"CONNOR," it shouted before I noticed it was just Jack Lozenge with many extra leaves taped to his clothes. "I need your help!"

"What do you want, Jack? Aren't you

satisfied? Isn't winning enough?"

"No! It isn't enough, apparently. The city is expecting me to make all of these financial decisions that I don't feel qualified to make. For God's sake, I'm the owner of a failing 3-ring binder company! I'm not cut out to handle the financials of an entire city! You have to help me, Connor. Please…"

I stopped walking and looked him in the eyes. "Fine. Let's do this."

EPILOGUE

So, you must be wondering where we all ended up. *How are Connor and Barcelona LaQuinta doing? Are Bartosz and Rebecca still on track for Med School? What ever happened to Gina?* You're probably screaming these questions at this book right now. Rest assured, I have provided you with the latest updates on our lives below:

Connor Gleim & Barcelona LaQuinta

As you can guess, I began taking care of the city's finances on Jack's behalf. While he held the title of 'City Comptroller' I did the actual work of one. I guess you could say I became a Comptroller's Comptroller. In exchange, Jack finally agreed to give up his title of Heir to the Airport Motel arm of LaQuinta. Me and Barcelona got married on the election stage moments before election night. We had a beautiful daughter who we named after Barcelona's great-grandmother: Margaret.

Bartosz Wiśniewski & Rebecca

Bartosz and Rebecca contacted Elias after the campaign concluded. He gave them glowing letters of recommendation when they applied to RowanSOM. Of course, they got accepted! Rebecca currently studies Advanced Medical Document Graphic Design while Bartosz studies Pediatrics.

Jack Lozenge & Montgomery O'Donnell

Jack Lozenge focuses full time on his company. He sold off the rest of his physical inventory and decided to create a Cloud-based service to support digital documentation and safe data. He teamed up with Montgomery's consulting firm to make it a success! As far as the town knows, he's still doing all of the work as City Comptroller. *wink*

Chalmers Topaz & Elias Loejzunjn

Chalmers and Elias were completely on board with Jack taking his company digital. Chalmers' stock in the company skyrocketed, and Elias got prime digital advertising for his Throat Lozenges. Elias eventually moved into town and they joined forces as the richest men in town. They got happily married (yeah, they're gay) and helped me ensure the city finances were in great shape.

Gina Canyon

Without the pressure of being the best Comptroller in the nation, Gina felt a sense of freedom. She bought an RV and saw every inch of the North American continent. She returned to town over a year later with amazing stories about all the sights she saw and people she met. With her was a man she met in Medicine Hat, Alberta. She is very happy.

ABOUT THE AUTHOR

Connor M. Gleim is a 39-year-old secret Comptroller residing with his wife Barcelona LaQuinta and their daughter Margaret. Unbeknownst to his constituents, he runs the famous City Comptroller position in their city on behalf the actual comptroller, Jack Lozenge. In his spare time, Connor likes to rate different brands of kale on YouTube, solve escape room puzzles in record time, and advocate for Cloud-based financial documentation.

www.ingramcontent.com/pod-product-compliance
Lightning Source LLC
Chambersburg PA
CBHW061734020426
42331CB00006B/1241